The
Life
and
Work
of

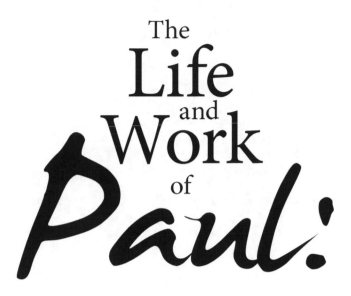

A Study Guide

RODNEY G. PETERS

WESTBOW
PRESS®
A DIVISION OF THOMAS NELSON
& ZONDERVAN

WestBow Press books may be ordered through booksellers or by contacting:

WestBow Press
A Division of Thomas Nelson & Zondervan
1663 Liberty Drive
Bloomington, IN 47403
www.westbowpress.com
844-714-3454

Because of the dynamic nature of the Internet, any web addresses or links contained in
this book may have changed since publication and may no longer be valid. The views
expressed in this work are solely those of the author and do not necessarily reflect the
views of the publisher, and the publisher hereby disclaims any responsibility for them.

Any people depicted in stock imagery provided by Getty Images are
models, and such images are being used for illustrative purposes only.
Certain stock imagery © Getty Images.

Scripture marked (NJB) taken from the New Jerusalem Bible. (C) Copyright
1985 by Darton, Longman, & Todd, Ltd. and Doubleday, a division of
Bantam Doubleday Dell Publishing Group, Inc. All rights reserved.

ISBN: 978-1-6642-3452-9 (sc)
ISBN: 978-1-6642-3454-3 (hc)
ISBN: 978-1-6642-3453-6 (e)

Library of Congress Control Number: 2021910004

Print information available on the last page.

WestBow Press rev. date: 6/21/2021

THE LIFE AND WORK OF PAUL: A STUDY GUIDE

Dora L. Dexter

Revised and updated
by
Rodney G. Peters

In memory of Dr. Dora Dexter

Within thirty years after Jesus died upon the Cross at Jerusalem,
Christianity was firmly established in the
very capital of the Roman Empire.
What were the great unifying forces which made that possible?
—Dora L. Dexter, MA, PhD (1958)

Foreword

This book is intended to offer the reader a close reading of the scripture, augmented with materials from outside the Bible in order to fill in some of the gaps and understand some of the context. The order is chronological insofar as there is general agreement, and the author takes responsibility for placing events and materials for which there is controversy. The whole work is an attempt to provide adult Bible study material which shares a lifelong love of scripture, along with the history and culture of its times. What an extraordinary experience it is to share the work of the person you have spent your love and life with. How marvelous to pass this work on to those who seek a deeper understanding of our Christian heritage.

Sandy Peters, in writing biographical information about her husband, gives us a glimpse into his own journey, into the soul of Rodney the searcher.

This book will give individuals and study groups fresh ideas and many opportunities for discussion. This foreword is an enticement to dig deeper into what will become a fulfilling experience for the reader of *The Life and Work of Paul, a Study Guide,* by Rodney G. Peters.

—Pat Tamburrino

Rodney Peters's Book on Paul

This book is dedicated to my husband, Rodney G. Peters (February 3, 1939–March 2, 2018), for his forty-nine years of faithful marriage, for love and care of his family, for more than sixty years of preaching (beginning as a youth pastor in rural Iowa churches), and for the completion of his calling to the ministry by serving two churches following his formal retirement.

Rodney began development of this work during the 1980s, but it waited in the wings. Occasionally I asked him how he was doing on the Paul book, but since his passion to serve was focused on care for his congregations, delivering the word, and doing community service, the completion of this book was set aside. Two months ago, I discovered it in his library, and I knew that this study of Paul was needed, to be a tool for the audiences it deserved.

Hence, I decided to follow through with what I knew to be true. My children think that "Dad left it for you to finish." Whether or not he did, it was clear that throughout the years Rodney's study of Paul never waned. Evidence of it was seen in details which Rodney incorporated into his sermons, lessons, and workshops. It is my hope that for you who wish to deepen your understanding of how Paul made Christendom alive, it is my honor to share the study guide on Paul, written by Rodney Peters.

Sandy Peters
September 8, 2020

Rodney Peters Biography

Rodney first worked in small churches in southwest Iowa in 1955, assisting an elder from Grace Presbyterian Church in Council Bluffs, who itinerated as a lay pastor. He never stopped serving congregations after that—graduating from Parsons College, Fairfield, Iowa, in 1961 and from McCormick Seminary, Chicago, Illinois, in 1965. Since then, his career has included large and small churches, a chaplaincy at Wichita Presbyterian Manor and Wesley Hospital, Wichita, Kansas, and a variety of denominational committee responsibilities.

Following McCormick, he was called to Jackson, Michigan, then back to Oak Park, Illinois for seven years, then to Clarksville, Iowa for another seven, next to Conway Springs and Wichita, Kansas for eleven years, and to Crane, Missouri for thirteen years. After retiring from full-time pastorates, he and his wife moved to Neosho, Missouri, where he took a part-time pastorate for eleven years at Bethany Church in Joplin, Missouri. He concluded his work at Bethany in August 2015, exactly sixty years after he began preaching. However, this retirement was short-lived, and two months later he was called to serve in Scammon, Kansas, until he became ill in December 2017.

He married Sandra Redmond Phillips in 1970. His own biography read, "We have four fantastic children with families, including five exciting young grandchildren. Our wonderful family is our proudest achievement. Sandy has spent the last ten years teaching at Crowder College in Neosho, in the fields of history, cultural diversity, and creative writing."

Rodney died peacefully, at Freeman Heart Institute, Joplin, Missouri on March 2, 2018. During those final days, he prayed aloud with his family and friends. One memorable prayer included his words, "I pray for all people, young and old." His future plans were stricken by his death, but being forward-looking, he had written: "Next, we plan to continue to travel, spend more time at a life-long interest in organic gardening, and pursue long-neglected interests—for me that will be to do some writing and woodworking. God has richly blessed us, and we look forward to the years ahead."

This short biography is dedicated to my husband, Rodney Gene Peters, for fulfilling his lifetime vocation to the ministry in Christian service. Rodney was a devoted husband and father to our children: Stephanie Lee (Phillips) Markstein, her husband, David, and their daughters Arielle and Mackenzie; Shannon Lee (Peters) Banks, her husband, Richard, and their daughter Maddie; Raleigh Gene Peters and his wife, Laura Leigh (Peelor) Peters; and Samantha Lee (Peters) Terrell, her husband, Joshua, and their sons Jennings and Sterling. Rodney and I were surrogate parents to Gordon Jack Welch, a high school member of Rodney's Oak Park Presbyterian Church Youth Group. As year-long sponsors in a Rotary program (Youth for Understanding), we hosted exchange students from Rauma, Finland, who were brothers: Ari, Risto, and Matti Nyfors. Another Youth for Understanding student, Ole Naesse, from Bergen, Norway, also lived with us. Katsuaki Otake, from my class at the Suzuki Institute,

Newman College (now Newman University) in Wichita, Kansas, and his wife Yumi, became part of our family. My father, L.W. (Pete) Redmond, as well as Stephanie's grandfather, Scott Phillips, shared our home.

Sandy Peters

Preface

In the beginning of a work such as this, it seems appropriate to review some assumptions about studying the Bible. Here are a few (probably not all) that are behind the present examination of Paul and his work.

1. Preparation. Maybe it is too obvious: serious Bible study needs to be undertaken prayerfully and as a process with some order. [For example, this book originated with a weekly, one-hour class of adults who very faithfully read ahead, attended regularly, and offered discussion. The series of classes opened with a video overview of Paul's missionary travels, which provided valuable preparation for the geography, breadth, and intensity of the events.] The beginning of any Bible study needs to include a measure of honesty about how little we know—or can know—of the times, places, and events recorded there. Finally, the best beginning acknowledges potential changes that may come into the lives of students when they open their hearts and spirits to the working of God.

2. First Reading. Pick one translation or version of the Bible that is your favorite. When you are assigned a passage, read it first from this Bible. Make notes if you usually do that. Look at the context if that helps you. Read the passage through and work to grasp its most apparent meaning.

3. Contemplation. Spend some time in serious thought about the significance of the passage and its impact on you, personally and spiritually. If the study is a group effort, let the contemplation be a combination of private reflection and group discussion. The purpose here is to assess the importance of the passage as you consider your past acquaintance with it or react to your first reading. We will consider history, culture, and religious significance later.

4. More Readings. Choose two or three other translations or versions of scripture, and read the passage from them. Compare the

wording and the meaning in such a way that you are satisfied with what the passage says. If there are divergent meanings or apparently uncertain wordings, you may want to consult a commentary or Bible dictionary. The purpose of this phase of your study is to arrive at a reasonable understanding of the literal content of the passage.

5. Analysis/Reflection.

Chapter 1
The Unifying Forces

I.   Political Influence: Roman Rule

    A. Under Roman domination, there was widespread peace under what was known as the Pax Romana, which lasted until about AD 100.

    B. How would the following produce a feeling of unity among the peoples of the Mediterranean world?
       1. Under Augustus, the Mediterranean world was at peace for many years.
       2. Much road building was done. "All roads led to Rome." A Roman army could, by forced march, reach any part of the empire in a week.
       3. Copies of Roman law were posted in the marketplace of every city and town in three languages.
       4. A man of any nationality could buy or earn Roman citizenship.

II.   Cultural Influence: Greek Culture and Language

    A. How did the Greeks contribute to the atmosphere of unity? Give examples from art, artifacts, and architecture commerce, shipping, and banking
       • philosophy, literature, and education

    B. Why was the earliest New Testament written in Greek?

    C. Why was the inscription that Pilate ordered put on the cross written in Latin, Hebrew, and Greek?

III.   Religious Influence: Roman and Hebrew
        A. What was emperor worship, and in what way could it serve
            as a unifying element?

        B. What do we mean by the phrase "Jews of the Dispersion?"

        C. How did the Jews keep their racial and religious integrity
            out in the empire?

        D. When Paul reached a new place, why would he always
            start his preaching in the synagogue?

IV.   Summary
        To what extent can it be said that the Romans, the Greeks, and
        the Hebrews prepared the way for the spread of Christianity in
        the Mediterranean world?

Chapter 2
The Preparation of Saul
Scripture References: Passim

I. Find the following facts about Saul:
    A. Birthplace: Acts 9:11; 21:39
    B. Nationality: 2 Corinthians 11:22; Philippians 3:5
    C. Ancestry (including Namesake): Philippians 3:5
    D. Religious Status: Acts 23:6
    E. Interest in Religion: Acts 22:3; Galatians 1:14
    F. Family: Acts 23:16
    G. Education (including Boyhood): Acts 22:3
    H. Relation to the Roman Empire: Acts 22:28
    I. Trade: Acts 18:3; 20:14
    J. Contacts with the New Faith: Acts 7:58; 8:1; Galatians 1:12

II. Describe the city of Tarsus and its life.

III. What influence would Saul's life in Tarsus have upon his character and his training?

IV. What effect would Saul's early religious training have upon his feeling for the new faith?

V. How would Saul's relation to the Roman Empire help him in his later work and travel?

VI. Why do you think Saul became a persecutor of the new faith?

Chapter 3
The Conversion
Scripture References: Acts 9, 22, and 26; Galatians 1

I.   Saul's contacts with the followers of Jesus prepare him for conversion.

   A. How would his part in the persecution of Christians affect his knowledge of Jesus?

   B. What effect would the death of Stephen have upon Saul?

   C. What did the new faith give that the Law could not give? (Also see Romans 7.)

II. Compare the three accounts in Acts of Saul's conversion experience.

   A. What time of day was it?

   B. What phenomena of nature were there?

   C. What did Saul do?

   D. What did the rest of the company do? (Compare passages.)

   E. How many heard the voice? (Compare passages.)

   F. What did the voice say?

   G. In what language did it speak?

   H. What happened to Saul?

I.   How did he reach Damascus?

I. Where did he stay?

J. How long was he blind?

K. Who received a vision about Saul?

L. Who else received a vision?

M. When did Saul receive his commission to witness for Christ?

II. Interpreting the Conversion of Saul

A. What would you say about this being literally a physical experience?

B. What would you say about this being a mental or psychological experience?

C. What would you say to a critic who claims this was merely a change of conviction or opinion about Jesus that was brought about by Saul's experience in persecution and his dissatisfaction with the Law?

D. How would you interpret the experience as a combination of these?

III. When Paul told the story of his experience, what one thing would people remember?

IV. Where did Saul go after his conversion?

V. Where did Saul begin preaching?

A. What effect did this have upon the Jews?

B. How did he escape from Damascus?

VI.   Who befriended Saul in Jerusalem?

    A. Why was he sent to Tarsus?

    B. What was the outcome of the relationship?

VII.   What did the conversion of Saul mean for the Christian faith?

Chapter 4
The Spread of the Gospel

Scripture References: Acts 8; 9:32–11:18

I.   The Gospel to the Samaritans

    A. Where was Philip's home?

    B. Where did Philip stop to preach on his way home?
       1. What was his success?
       2. Who tried to buy the power of "speaking in tongues"?

    C. What effect did Philip's work here have on the apostles in Jerusalem?
       1. Who were sent to investigate, and what was their decision?
       2. What did they do with the converts?
       3. Who were the converts, and how were they related to the Jews?

    D. Is the faith strictly Jewish now?

    E. Did the apostles in Jerusalem understand at this time that Christianity was to become a universal religion?

II. The Gospel for the Ethiopian Eunuch

    A. What was unusual about this eunuch?

    B. What was the eunuch doing when Philip found him?
       1. What was the significance of the passage?
       2. What were the followers of Jesus trying to prove from this passage?

C. How would the conversion of the eunuch change the early church?

III.   The Gospel at Joppa and Caesarea

A. Who was the evangelist for these cities?

B. What two miracles did he perform near the seacoast?

C. With whom did he stay at Joppa?
    1. What was his host's occupation, and where did he live?
    2. How did the Jews feel about men with this occupation?

D. Review the evangelist's dream, and explain the meaning of the dream
    •   in light of the immediate situation of the meal in the host's home; and
    •   in light of the situation soon to face the early church.

E. Who and where was Cornelius, and how did he hear about Jesus?

F. What success did Peter have in his preaching in Caesarea?

G. Explain the positive and negative reactions when Peter reported in Jerusalem.

H. What are the national origins of the groups converted by Philip and Peter, and what is the significance of those three groups?

I. Did the apostles at Jerusalem realize yet that the gospel of Jesus was for all people?

Chapter 5
The Door Opens Wider
Scripture Reference: Acts 11:19–12:25

I.   The Gospel for the Greeks

    A. How far did the disciples (who were scattered by the persecution following the death of Stephen) travel?

    B. What care did these men take in their preaching?

    C. What departure from this policy was made in Antioch?

    D. Who was Barnabas, and why would he be chosen to assume responsibility in Antioch?

    E. Whom did Barnabas choose to help him in Antioch?
      1. Pick up the story from when Saul was converted.
      2. What is suggested about Paul's possible activity after he left Jerusalem?

    F. When and by whom do you think the churches mentioned in Acts 15:41 were founded?

    G. Who was the second known martyr for the new faith?

    H. Tell the circumstances under which he was martyred.

    I. Who was expected to be the third martyr?
      1. Tell the story of his escape.
      2. Who do you think the "messenger of the Lord" might have been?

    J. What was the occasion for Saul and Barnabas to travel to Jerusalem?

II.   The Encounter with the Mysteries

As the door of the new faith opened a bit wider, its proponents had to confront more fully the other religions of their time. There was a diminishing set of ancient institutions because the weaknesses and philosophical inadequacies of the "old gods" had become apparent. They were being replaced by mystery religions that attempted to explain life and provide new worship activities for a modern era. The central similarity of the mysteries was the secret ceremony based on secret meanings of the old myths. Each offered followers a part of limited access to future life, which brought peace to this life. In cultures with little present hope, the mysteries presented a way out of human miseries. A sampling of the mystery religions will serve as explanation of this "worldwide" phenomenon. Here are reviews of one each from Greece, Phrygia, Thrace, Persia, and Egypt.

1. The Eleusinian mysteries of Greece revolved around Demeter, the goddess of soil and grain. Demeter's daughter, Persephone, was taken away into Hades by Pluto. She was only allowed to come back for eight months of the year. During the four months of her absence, there was winter. The women being initiated into this religion brought pigs for sacrifice. They engaged in ritual bathing and then formed a procession to travel to Eleusis (thirteen miles from Attica), where there was a cane with a stalk of grain in it. This was the symbol of the religion, and the initiates were then given stalks of grain as symbols of their faith. Completing the rituals and displaying the symbols of the faith aided in freeing Persephone, bringing the end of winter and providing for a new crop, thus ensuring the future of human life.

2. Phrygia's Cybele and Attis cult worshipped Cybele, Asia Minor's goddess of wild nature. Cybele mourned the death of Attis, a male god, until he rose from death in the spring, bringing new life and the promise of an unending future. In Roman mythology, Cybele was worshipped as the mother of the gods, and a temple was built for her. The symbol of this mystery was a large meteoric stone, and the ceremony of the religion centered around the raising of Attis from

the dead. The worshippers believed their praise of his triumph would give them a similar resurrection.

3. A representative mystery from Thrace worshipped Dionysus, the god of the vine. Several myths grew up around Dionysus, including one which claimed that he was captured as a child by some sailors as he wandered along the sea, but he was saved by vines which grew around the ship and kept it from leaving shore. Early in its development, the ritual of this mystery included an orgy in which worshipers ate the raw flesh and drank the warm blood of the sacrificial goat. They drank wine until they entered a drunken frenzy, during which they believed Dionysus was within them. Later in its history, the cult orgies dissolved into more sober and speculative devotion. The worshipers were promised a blessed immortality and given passwords for entrance into the nether world.

4. Mithraism, a Persian mystery religion, was the last to become popular in Rome. It was the most popular too, being spread in and by the Roman army. The worship of Mithras, god of light and truth and opponent of darkness and evil, was the first to exclude women. It became popular with the soldiers, probably because Mithras was a hero god. This mystery religion gave Christianity the most trouble as a rival because of a surprising similarity of symbols and characteristics. Both religions were based on individual choice. Both employed an emotional, mystical experience. The concept of salvation was similar in both. Among other similarities: baptism, the sign of the cross, a feast of bread and wine, an ascension into heaven, and the continuance of blessings from heaven. Mithras was a hero deity who had been a servant of mankind on earth, thus being able to help humanity to an immortal life.

Initiation into the cult was an elaborate and painful process of ablutions, rites, and sacred meals, necessary to pass through each of seven stages—corresponding to seven heavens. Gathering places for Mithraism were often underground and were called speloea. They were seldom large but were numerous, especially in some cities and provinces. Common to all of them was a relief depicting Mithras killing a bull. It was the same type of art and very similar in all the places of worship. Hardly anything is known of the actual myths and mysteries of this religion.

5. In the Osiris-Isis Cult of Egypt, the goddess of fertility (Isis) grieved the death of Osiris and finally recovered his body, restored him to life, and made him king of the nether world. Osiris had been a king of Egypt who had bestowed gifts on mankind, so he would be expected to go to the home of the blest after death and to assure worshipers of a blessed immortality with him. Initiation into the cult followed the usual procedure of purification rites and fasting, which led to a mystical religious experience. This experience was believed to create a union between the worshipper and the deity, which assured a happy afterlife.

Ultimately, Christianity became more satisfying than any of the ancient religions—even as they were turned into mystery cults. Christian faith blossomed and grew as they waned and finally disappeared.

III.

    A. What do we mean by the Mystery Religions?

    B. What brought the Mysteries into existence?

    C. Describe the following Mysteries, including the gods they worshipped, the representation, and the location where the Mystery originated.
       1. The Eleusinian Mysteries
       2. The Cybele and Attis Cult
       3. The Dionysus Cult
       4. Mithraism
       5. The Osiris–Isis Cult

    D. Explain any similarities between early Christianity and the Mysteries.

Chapter 6
The First Missionary Campaign
Scripture Reference: Acts 13:1–14:28

I. The Beginning of Missionary Outreach

    A. The interest of the book of Acts now shifts:
        1. From what city to what city?
        2. From what ethnic group to what ethnic group?
        3. From what individual man to what individual man?

    B. Who were sent out as commissioned evangelists for the new faith?
        1. Who accompanied them?
        2. For what purpose?

    C. Who apparently took the lead at the beginning of the trip?

II. First Steps

    A. To what island did they go?

    B. Why would they go there?

    C. What do you think was the first important place visited?
        1. What happened there?
        2. Why did they leave?

    D. Who took the lead from this time on—and under what name?

III. Further Steps

    A. What happened at Perga?

B. Where did Paul make his first contacts in Antioch of Pisidia?
   1. What success did Paul have?
   2. Why did Paul and Barnabas leave town?

C. Relate the incident at Lystra.
   1. Why were Barnabas and Paul taken to be Jupiter and Mercury?
   2. What did the people of Lystra try to do for Paul and Barnabas?
   3. What was the end result?

IV. On a map, find the places visited on this journey, and trace the line of travel.

Chapter 7
The Council at Jerusalem
Scripture Reference: Acts 15; Galatians 2

I. Questions about gentiles in the Antioch Church

    A. What specific concern arose in the Antioch Church?

    B. Describe the feeling Jews had for gentiles.

    C. What might be the results of such feelings?

    D. What did gentile Christians think made them part of the new faith?

    E. What did Jews expect would be a part of the gentile Christian's faith?

II. Prelude to the Council at Jerusalem

    A. What question was it obvious that Christianity had to answer?

    B. Who raised the issue at Antioch?

    C. Who were selected to go to Jerusalem? For what purpose?

III. What young man did Paul take with him? Why?

    A. What was his nationality?

    B. What was the outcome of his attending?

IV. The Council at Jerusalem

    A. Make a list of the twelve who were present.

B. Summarize the proceedings.
   1. Who were the prominent speakers?
   2. What decision was reached?
   3. What does Paul (in Galatians) say resulted?
   4. Upon what basis could a gentile become a Christian in the future?
   5. What four requirements were made? Toward what end?
   6. Were there any requirements about Temple worship?

C. What agreement did Paul make with the leaders at Jerusalem?

D. What incident in Galatians 2 shows that the question was not entirely settled?

E. Who returned to Antioch with Paul to confirm the decision of the Council?

Chapter 8
The Second Missionary Campaign
Antioch to Philippi
Scripture Reference: Acts 15:36–16:40

I.   A Change of Partnerships

    A. Why did Paul and Barnabas part company at the beginning of this campaign?

    B. Did Paul always have this feeling toward Mark? (2 Timothy 4:11; Colossians 4:10; Philemon 33)

    C. Whom did Paul choose at Lystra to perform the kind of work previously done by John Mark?

    D. What do we know about this young man and his family? (2 Timothy 1:5)

II.   A Change of Plans

    A. After a time of visiting and consolidating established churches in Asia Minor, where did Paul plan to go?

    B. Why did he change his plans and what name does the change lend to this campaign?

    C. What important city on the coast did Paul reach?

    D. What experience did he have there?

    E. Are there any clues about it in Acts 16:10?

    F. Who apparently joined Paul there?

III. The First Major Stop on the Second Campaign: Philippi

    A. What clue in Acts 16 suggests that there were few Jews in Philippi?

    B. Who was Paul's first convert in Philippi?

    C. What service did she render Paul and his company?

    D. Relate the story of healing the slave girl.

    E. What accusation was made against Paul by the girl's masters?

    F. What was the real reason for their anger?

    G. What was done to Paul and Silas?

    H. Describe the unusual experience during the night.

IV. Paul and the Magistrates of Philippi

    A. Why did the magistrates send word to the jailer to let these men go free?

    B. Note the change of pronouns in Acts 16:16–17 and 19–34.

    C. Who of Paul's company is at large and might be influential?

    D. What did Paul demand of the magistrates?

    E. What made the magistrates accede to Paul's demands?

    F. Did Paul hurry from the city?

    G. Whom did Paul apparently leave in Philippi, and what is the clue?

    H. When did the separation probably take place?

Chapter 9
The Second Missionary Campaign
Thessalonica and Athens
Scripture Reference: Acts 17

After traveling from the coastal town of Neapolis, through two towns where there was no Jewish synagogue (Amphipolis and Apollonia), Paul and Silas (and maybe Timothy) arrived in Thessalonica and went immediately to the synagogue to begin three Sabbaths of teaching and preaching. It was here that they made their first contact with Jews in the Macedonia of Paul's vision. The work seems to have been successful, since there were enough responding to make the Jews furious. One of the converts in Thessalonica was probably Aristarchus, who became one of Paul's most faithful companions (20:4; Colossians 4:10). No doubt, most of those converted were gentiles, both those who had embraced Judaism and those who had not.

Paul and Silas did not remain long in Thessalonica, because of the opposition of the Jewish community. While there, they stayed with a man named Jason (probably also referred to in Romans 16:21), who opened his house to the gathering of new Christians. Paul paid for his keep through his work—probably tent making—and the contributions of others, including the Philippians (2 Thessalonians 3:7ff; Philippians 4:16). The controversial team left quickly, in the night, with the help of members of the new faith and went directly to the synagogue in Beroea. The persecution continued in Thessalonica, however, and leaders of the gathering were hauled into the presence of the city council (see also 1 Thessalonians 2:14). They had to "post bail" before they could go free.

The Jews in Beroea welcomed Paul's preaching and studied the scriptures with him. The major results were that many believed the Christian message and that the Jews in Thessalonica soon heard of it and came to stir up trouble. Therefore, Paul was whisked away to the coast, leaving Silas and Timothy behind. They escorted him as far as Athens, where he waited for Silas and Timothy to join him. While there, he occupied his time by arguing in the synagogue and the market place, trying to rid the city of idols. He joined in the debates at the Areopagus, a hill where the high court convened. For Paul, it was the most impressive place in Athens because there the people spent all their time "telling or hearing something new." Today the Areopagus is still there, but the activities of ancient Greek culture are gone, including the idols Paul preached against.

Paul finally took his defense of the Christian faith to the Athenian high court itself. He made contact with his listeners by noting a monument he had seen which was inscribed, "To an Unknown God." His speech may be outlined as follows:

1. God does not live in shrines
    a. God is not served by human hands
       (1) God gives everything to all people
       (2) God made all people to live on earth
    b. God is not far from each one of us
2. Being God's offspring, we ought not to think of God like gold, silver, or stone.
    a. God calls everyone to repent
    b. God has fixed a day of judgment
    c. The world will be judged by a resurrected man (Jesus)

At the mention of the resurrection of the dead, the Athenians lost interest because the majority of them did not accept it.

Two of the major philosophical schools active in Athens during the first century were Stoicism and Epicureanism. Stoicism was founded by Zeno shortly after 300 BCE. The name comes from the Greek word for "porch"—from which Zeno taught. Stoicism was the most vigorous of all the post Aristotelian schools of philosophy. It was divided into three sections: logic, physics, and ethics. The Stoic logic (theory of knowledge) was based on the belief that the "forms" of Plato are merely mental concepts. Physics basically consisted of the idea that only matter is real. It was in the field of ethics that Stoicism made its only original philosophical assertion: that the highest good for any creature is acting in accord with its nature.

Epicurus (341–270 BCE) founded the philosophy bearing his name, which descended from Greek Atomism. It held that the goal of human life should be maximum pleasure, and that pleasure should be regulated by morality, temperance, serenity, and cultural development. The Epicurean philosophical ethics eliminated all belief in divine causality because it stimulated painful emotions of fear and insecurity. Epicurus advocated frugality, modesty, simplicity, and justice: themes which would later be seen in the writings of Christian asceticism.

The named converts from Paul's work in Athens are Dionysius the Areopagite and a woman named Damaris. Others are reported to have converted with them. But there is no sign of great success in Paul's work at Athens, and he later changes his approach completely. He vows not to mingle Christian theology and philosophy, saying he "will know only Christ, and him crucified."

I. Thessalonica

    A. Where in Thessalonica did Paul make his first contact with the Jews?

    B. What success did he have?

    C. How long did he stay?

    D. With whom did Paul stay while in Thessalonica?

    E. How did Paul finance himself?
       (2 Thessalonians 3:7ff; Philippians 4:16)

    F. Under what circumstances did Paul leave Thessalonica?

    G. Who was implicated in these circumstances?

    H. How did Paul leave Thessalonica and where did he go?

I. What did Paul do in this new location?

J. What were the two major results?

II.   Athens

    A. For whom was Paul waiting in Athens?

    B. How did he occupy his time?

    C. What was the most impressive thing about Athens in Paul's day?

    D. What would you expect to find in Athens today?

    E. Where did Paul make his defense of the new faith?

    F. How did he make a point of contact with his listeners?

    G. Outline Paul's speech to the Athenians.

    H. What made the Athenians lose interest?

    I. Name and describe two great schools of philosophy which existed in Athens at the time of Paul.

    J. What converts did Paul make in Athens?

Chapter 10
The Second Missionary Campaign
Corinth to Jerusalem
Scripture Reference: Acts 18:1–23

When Paul got to Corinth, he confronted a totally different group of people. Those in Athens had been non-Jewish, had been more philosophical in approach than religious, and had begun with a more skeptical attitude. Athens was the center of education and government for the nation.

In Corinth, Paul was speaking to Jews who worshipped in a synagogue, lived by the cultural and religious standards of Judaism, and were not worshipers of idols. Corinth was at the center of commercial and religious interchange for Greece. It was a truly cosmopolitan city

I.   Corinth

    A. How did Corinth differ from Athens?

    B. With whom and how did Paul occupy his time in Corinth?

    C. What difference did the coming of Timothy and Silas make in the work at Corinth?
             (2 Corinthians 11:9)

    D. What was Paul's attitude toward the Jews in Corinth?

    E. Where did Paul and his Christian converts meet?

    F. What converts did Paul make in Corinth?

    G. How long did Paul remain in Corinth?

    H. How did the Jews attempt to ruin Paul?

       1. Who was Gallio?

       2. What accusations did the Jews bring against Paul?

       3. Why was Gallio not interested?

       4. What indignity did Gallio permit?

II.   The End of the Second Missionary Campaign

     A. What connection did Paul have with Cenchreae?

     B. Who accompanied Paul to Ephesus?

     C. What impression did the preaching of Paul make upon the people at Ephesus?

     D. When leaving Ephesus, where did Paul go?

     E. What two stops did he apparently make on the way?

     F. Where was the "Church" mentioned in 18:22?

     G. Where did the Second Missionary Campaign end?

III.   On a map trace Paul's line of travel, and list the places visited on this journey.

IV.   Note Paul's work immediately following the conclusion of this campaign.

Chapter 11
The Writings of Paul
Scripture Reference: Your favorite of Paul's writings

The differences between "letters" and "epistles" are largely semantic and academic. Modern usage makes epistle a sarcastic remark, even though the older definition is still acceptable: a long, formal, didactic (teaching) letter. Its root (stellein) gives us "summons," and the intent of epistles is often hortatory, whether ancient or modern. By contrast, a letter is usually understood in a much more straightforward manner: a written or printed message of a direct personal or business nature written to an individual or body.

Paul's writings have some characteristics of both and are difficult to classify clearly. They typically get the heading "letters" in modern commentaries and translations because they are not literary productions, and they most often address issues of a personal nature to Paul or the communities/Christians he addresses. The collection of Paul's writings does not provide a systematic discussion of his theology or beliefs. They are based on his preaching in the places where he later sends letters. Therefore, the writings are a mix of various forms. One might analyze individual writings and choose to designate each as epistle or letter, depending on the content and style. The more practical way of addressing the issue is to call them all letters and be done with it.

The important concern for most Bible students revolves around the value of the writings of Paul to the individual Christian and to the church. The chief reason for studying these writings (letters) is three-pronged. First, they show us something of the life and problems of the early congregations and Christians, so they are important historical documents. Second, they contain a faithful apostle's prayerful advice for his contemporaries—both individuals and communities, so they are important religious documents. Third, since we face many similar problems in the modern era, they become important spiritual documents for us and for our churches, offering a kind of perspective not frequently available in our own culture.

Unfortunately, we are missing some of the writings of Paul, even though we know they existed at one time, because he refers to some in the writings we do have. For example, in First Corinthians he refers to an earlier letter to that church. We probably have little, if any, of that writing or others that we may speculate were written. What we do have is some notion of the way Paul wrote, as seen in The Introduction to Paul in the *New Jerusalem Bible*. The letters generally considered to be authored by Paul are the following: Romans, Corinthians (2), Colossians, Philippians, Thessalonians (2), Philemon, Ephesians, Galatians, Titus, and Timothy (2). Only a few scholars give Paul credit for writing Hebrews, and the arguments against that are strong enough to convince this author. There may also be fragments of letters imbedded in the writings we do possess, but they are nearly impossible to separate and will not be considered as independent, even if they actually exist.

Paul corresponded in writing for a very modern reason. He received news of his friends and churches by travelers and business people using the Roman roads to cross and re-cross the Northern Mediterranean world. When he heard particularly disturbing or very exciting news, his impulse was to visit. However, Paul was realistic about the limits of his age, so he would dictate a letter to a scribe, who would put it in writing and bring it to Paul for a few final words and greetings. In this way he could address special concerns (for example, the matter of Philemon's runaway slave, Onesimus) without being physically present (for the reunion). He could also address a variety of problems in an efficient and personal manner, without the risk of personal rancor if he were to visit.

Frequent, fairly inexpensive letters were made possible by the use of papyrus, the most common form of paper in Paul's day. It had been in existence for some time, and would remain a primary communications tool for many years. A huge collection of papyrus letters, called the Papyri, tells much about ancient life and includes most of Paul's writings. It was through the analysis of the Papyri that Adolph Deissmann found the key to the New Testament language.

I.   What are the characteristics of an epistle?

II.   What are the characteristics of a letter?

III.   Are Paul's writings letters or epistles?

IV.   Why are Paul's writings valuable?
        A. Do we have all of them?

        B. How do we know?

        C. List the names of thirteen that we have.

V.   Why did Paul correspond in writing?

VI.   What are the Papyri?
        A. What is of interest about them?

        B. Give an account of Papyri discoveries.

        C. What relation do the Papyri have to the New Testament?

VII.   What is your favorite writing of Paul?

        A. Describe it and tell what is important about it.

        B. How does it relate to other writings of the Bible?

        C. What kind of person does this writing show Paul to be?

Chapter 12
The Letters to the Thessalonians
Scripture Reference: 1 and 2 Thessalonians

Early in the history of Jewish thought it became common to refer to the end of time when the Jews would be rewarded for injustices they had suffered, while those who oppressed them would be punished. The instrument for accomplishing such an end would be one chosen by God—a Messiah.

This standard resolution for the problem of good and evil in the world was an important part of prophetic, apocalyptic, and eschatological literature. The view became popular and was widely distributed toward the end of the Old Testament period and during the time between the Old and New Testaments.

Jewish prophets (Daniel first, but also Isaiah and Micah) spoke of a single person as Messiah. He would be of the house of David and in a peculiar father-son relationship with God. He would do all God's will; his rule would be one of absolute righteousness; he would compel all to honor the God of Israel; and he would bestow on his people perfect peace and happiness forever. In the Messiah, earlier promises of God concerning the expansion and unity of Israel would come to fruition. Long before New Testament times, belief in and expectation of a Messiah became an article of faith for the vast majority of Jews. They assumed his coming would be unexpected and mysterious, and it was a common belief that the Messiah would perform signs and wonders (miracles).

Over the years there was continual change in the concept of this Messiah. With the development of eschatological doctrine, the picture of the Messiah became more detailed and involved. They nearly always expected a political deliverer, however, not a religious or spiritual one. Jesus's early popularity derived largely from the anticipation that he might well be that political deliverer. As his ministry progressed, it became more and more apparent that he had no political aspirations, and many people either lost interest or refused to believe he had any special message for Judaism.

Jesus failed to liberate them from the Romans (as Judas Maccabeus had done in 165 BC). He had not tried to set up a Jewish state. And when he was killed, they then expected him to return in glory, to deliver judgment, and to create the final political kingdom. They called him the Christ (the Greek equivalent of Messiah) because they thought he was the anointed one of God, destined to create the glorious and triumphant Jewish kingdom.

All this weight of material and human hope was present during the early church's life and development. There were different interpretations, but the basic expectation was present in the private theology of most followers of Jesus, who continued with the new faith after the resurrection. It was certainly a part of the life of the congregation in Thessalonica from which Timothy brought news to Paul while he was in Athens or Corinth.

The believers in Thessalonica had begun to follow blindly after the Judean churches, thus adopting their problems and errors. Paul wanted to visit Thessalonica, but he was "hindered by Satan." Therefore, he had to write a letter to help them address their troubles. Paul had left the city by night in the face of danger and persecution, so the letter seemed the best alternative.

Evidently, there were serious disagreements—and perhaps divisions—among the Thessalonians over morality and over the resurrection. The morality issue is addressed briefly early in chapter 4, but they had bigger problems with understanding what would happen to believers who died before the Messiah returned. Paul tries to address this issue from the point of view of Jesus's own teachings (Matthew 25:32ff). He follows that with his own view of the end of time. *The New Jerusalem Bible* (Doubleday, 1985) footnote on the passage says,

Of all the details given here: that the dead will answer the summons by returning to life, that they and the living will be taken to meet the Lord, and that they will accompany him to the judgment with which the eternal kingdom begins, the essential one is the last: eternal life with Christ … That is to be the "salvation," the "glory," the "kingdom" that Jesus shares among his chosen followers. (p. 1955)

Out of such a heavily eschatological interpretation comes a series of exhortations about how to prepare for the meeting of the Messiah on the "Day of the Lord" (judgment day), or when Jesus returns. It is apparent from the earlier passage (v. 17, "we") that Paul expects this to happen during his own lifetime.

It seems that the second letter to Thessalonica was written soon after the first, with two new purposes: to respond to others who had been writing under his name, and to clarify misconceptions about the "second coming." On the issue of misrepresented writings, Paul refers to them directly in 2 Thessalonians 2:2–3 and 3:2, urging the people to persevere in the teachings Paul himself has presented.

Regarding misinterpretations of his teaching about the Day of the Lord, Paul has more to say. William Barclay has written, "The first letter insists that the Day of the Lord will come like a thief in the night, and urges watchfulness (1 Thessalonians 5:2; 5:6). But this had produced an unhealthy situation where men did nothing but watch and wait; and in the second letter Paul explains that signs must come first before the Second Coming should come (2 Thessalonians 2–12)." (Westminster, 1959, *The Letters to the Philippians, Colossians, and Thessalonians*: p. 215)

Apparently there were also those who had adopted a lifestyle of pure laziness, living off the work of others. Paul speaks to this misreading of his first letter very forcefully. In 2 Thessalonians 3:10 he says, "We urged you when we were with you not to let anyone eat if he refused to work." (NJB). This may have been from Jesus's teaching but more likely was simply a popular saying adapted to Christian life. It has been repeated often in history, as by John Smith who gave the command, "He who does not work shall not eat," to the people of the early American colonies.

While much of the second letter repeats viewpoints from the first, Paul does indicate a change of attitude about the imminence of the second coming. He gives more instructions for preparation and for life together that seem to be longer-term concerns. He repeats Jesus's own injunction that the coming will be unexpected, without such immediate force as in the first letter.

The authenticity of this letter being important, Paul points out his common practice of writing a closing greeting in his own hand (v. 17). It probably was not unique to this letter but needed to be pointed out here. Timothy served as Paul's secretary during this time and would have been responsible for all the writing except the final benediction.

I.   Discuss the Messianic hope of the Jews, including its origin and development.

II.   For what were the Jews of Jesus's time looking?

III.   What made Jesus so popular at the beginning of his career and so unpopular as his ministry advanced?

    A. What had Jesus failed to do?

    B. What did his followers expect him to do in the near future?

    C. Why did the followers call him Jesus Christ?

IV.   Where was Paul when he wrote the letters to the Thessalonians?

    A. Who had brought him greetings and news from the church there?

    B. What was happening to the Christians at Thessalonica? (1 Thessalonians 2:14)

    C. Why did Paul write instead of going? (1 Thessalonians 2:18)

    D. Why had Paul left Thessalonica earlier?

V.   From 1 Thessalonians 4:13–18, what would you think was the problem which faced the church at Thessalonica?

VI. What connection to the exhortations in 1 Thessalonians 5:12–22 have with the coming of Christ?

VII. What indications do we have in 2 Thessalonians 2 and 3 that false letters purporting to be from Paul were being circulated in the area?

VIII. How were the people of the church behaving in anticipation of the speedy return of Christ?

    A. Why did Paul give the advice found in 2 Thessalonians 3:10?

    B. Do you know any other historical instances in which this command was issued?

    C. In what terms does Paul express his belief that the return of Christ would not be immediate?

IX. How does Paul insure the genuineness of his letters in 2 Thessalonians 3:17?

X. Who evidently transcribed these letters for Paul?

Chapter 13
The Third Missionary Campaign
Paul in Ephesus Again
Scripture Reference: Acts 18:24–20:1

A considerable "Christian" presence existed in Ephesus by the time Paul arrived on his second visit. Much of the vitality of that community of the new faith depended on Apollos, a brilliant Jew from Alexandria, Egypt, who had been converted and trained as a teacher. When he arrived in Ephesus, he began preaching and teaching in the synagogue. He told of the coming of the Messiah from the point of view of John the Baptist, as though the event were not yet complete. It seems possible that Apollos may have been baptized by John.

Priscilla and Aquila heard him and concluded they needed to "set him right" by sharing the story of the life, teaching, death, and resurrection of Jesus. Apparently, that encouraged Apollos to go on a preaching and teaching campaign into Greece (Achaia, including Corinth). For that trip, he was encouraged by Aquila and Priscilla as well as the leaders (brothers) of the Ephesian church. He was sent off with a letter of reference, which would assure him of a good reception when he met the Christians in the Greek province of Achaia.

Paul was anxious to return to Ephesus and take up his work there because it had been cut short on his first visit and because he had heard that the believers there had not received the Holy Spirit. It was his intent to review and correct the preaching of Apollos, along with preaching himself, so that the people might receive the baptism of the Holy Spirit, as had been the case in other places where he had worked. After confirming the message of Aquila and Priscilla by preaching about Jesus, the Holy Spirit was visited upon the believers.

On this trip to Ephesus, Paul was with the community of believers for a lengthy stay. He preached at the synagogue in Ephesus for three months, as compared to the synagogues of other cities, where he preached from one time to several Sabbaths. However, he was finally driven out, and when his welcome ended at the synagogue, he went to the Hall of Tyrannus, where he preached and taught for two years.

The people of Ephesus began to view Paul as a magician. Because he was so successful, a Jewish chief priest tried to exorcise an evil spirit by calling on the names of Jesus and Paul. The evil spirit answered saying, "Jesus I know, and Paul I know, but who are you?" The man with the spirit attacked them, and they ran from the house naked and beaten. All of Ephesus heard about the incident. Magicians burned their books (worth fifty thousand pieces of silver) in public, renounced the art of magic, and accepted the Lord.

Ephesus was home to one of the seven wonders of the ancient world: the Temple of Diana. The other wonders were the pyramids of Egypt, the hanging gardens of Babylon, Phidias's statue of Zeus, the tomb of Mausolus, the Colossus of Rhodes, and Pharos at Alexandria, Egypt.

Ephesus also boasted the temple of the Gordian Knot up to the time of Alexander the Great. This knot had been tied by the King of Phrygia, and it was widely believed that it would only be untied by a person who would conquer all of Asia. Alexander the Great cut it with his sword.

I.   Background: Describe the experience of Apollos in Ephesus.

    A. Who was Apollos?

    B. Where was he from?

    C. What was his religion?

    D. If he was a follower of John the Baptist, what would be his message?

    E. Where did Apollos preach?

II.   What did Aquila and Priscilla add to the message of Apollos when they "set him right"?

III.   What was there about Ephesus which made Paul anxious to preach there?

A. What did Paul find it necessary to correct from the work of Apollos?

B. How long did Paul preach in the synagogue of Ephesus?
1. Compare this with other cities.
2. Where did he preach when he had been driven from the synagogue?
3. For how long?

IV. What belief arose in Ephesus concerning Paul's power to perform miracles?

A. Who tried to exert Paul's power to cast out demons?

B. With what result?

C. What was the effect of Paul's preaching on the practice of magic?

V. List the seven wonders of the ancient world.

VI. The Gordian Knot was kept in Ephesus up to the time of Alexander the Great.

A. What was this knot?

B. How did Alexander cope with it?

VII. Tell about the trouble Paul had with the silversmiths.

A. Why didn't Paul appeal to the people?

B. Who made an unsuccessful attempt to appeal to them?

C. How was the trouble finally ended?

VIII. What was the result of Paul's work in Ephesus?

Chapter 14
Paul's Letter to the Galatians
Scripture Reference: Galatians

I.   To whom was the letter to the Galatians written?

II.   Scholars have two theories about Galatia, the North Galatian Theory and the South Galatian Theory. Explain each.

III. Who was destroying the work of Paul in Galatia? How?

IV.   Find the following in Paul's answer to those who attacked his apostleship: (Galatians 1 and 2)

   A. From whom did he claim to have received his apostleship?

   B. How does he show that he had no opportunity to receive his apostleship from the Apostles in Jerusalem:
   1. —before his conversion? (Galatians 1:11–17)
   2. —after his return from Damascus? (Galatians 1:18–24)

   C. When the question of gentiles in the new faith arose, how did Paul rank with the Apostles? (Galatians 2)

   D. What other incident in chapter 2 speaks to his relationship with them? Explain.

V.   What indication is there in chapter 1 of an attack upon the character of Paul? In chapter 4?

VI.   In what chapters does Paul prove that his ministry has the authority of the Jewish scriptures behind it?

VII. Which does Paul say came first, the Law or the Promise?

A. How much time elapsed between them?

B. Did the Law erase the Promise?

C. What was the purpose of the Law?

D. What was the duty of the Greek pedagogue?

E. In what way was the Law similar?

F. In what way was an underage heir bound by the Law?

G. What in the religious life was the equivalent of "coming of age"?

VIII. In the chapter 4:21–31 reference the family of Abraham, who are symbolized:

A. —by Hagar?

B. —by Sarah?

IX. How had the idea that the Christian was "free" been abused in Galatia?

X. What warning did Paul give?

Chapter 15
Paul's Correspondence with Corinth
Scripture Reference: 1 and 2 Corinthians, passim

An Outline of 1 Corinthians

I. Introduction
    A. Address and salutation
    B. Thanksgiving

II. The Problem of Factions
    A. Argument against factions
    B. Other considerations

III. Moral Standards of the Christian Life
    A. Problems of sex and property
    B. Problems of marriage and celibacy

IV. Christian Freedom
    A. Food offered to idols
    B. Paul's renunciation of rights
    C. The peril of the strong
    D. Statement of principles

V. Worship
    A. The veiling of women
    B. The Lord's Supper
    C. Spiritual gifts

VI. Resurrection of the Dead
    A. Jesus's resurrection
    B. The eschatological drama
    C. The resurrection body
    D. Christian confidence

VII.   Personal Matters
       A. Contributions
       B. Travel plans

VIII. Closing and benediction

I.   How many letters to Corinth do we apparently have in the New Testament?

       A. How many do the Biblical scholars think there were?

       B. List the letters.

II.   From what place were the first two letters written?

       A. The third?

       B. Subsequent letters?

III.   In 1 Corinthians 5:9, find a purpose for writing the first letter.

IV.   What purpose for the second letter to Corinth (our 1 Corinthians) do you find in:

       A. 1:11 (Who were the people mentioned here?)

       B. 5:1

       C. 7:1

       D. 16:12

       E. 16:17

V.   Who evidently carried this letter to Corinth? (Chapters 4:17 and 16:10[?])

VI. First Corinthians has been compared to a well-kept park, Second Corinthians to a trackless forest. Why?

VII. In 2 Corinthians 2:4 and 7:8, Paul refers to a severe letter to Corinth which caused him tears and regret ... 2:9 refers to it as a "showdown."

    A. What is that letter?

    B. What arguments are there in favor of this being the bitter letter?

    C. Who evidently carried this bitter letter? (Chapters 2 and 7)

VIII. Make a brief outline of 1 Corinthians.

Chapter 16
Paul's Advice to the Corinthians
Scripture Reference: 1 Corinthians 1–6

Having received word of difficulties at the church in Corinth, Paul has prepared a careful and definitive guide for the congregation. The first six chapters specifically address the issues that have come to his attention through friends or concerned elders. The remainder of the letter, which will be studied in subsequent chapters, addresses questions asked by the church in a more formal way.

I.   I Factions in the Church (Chapters 1–4)

    A. What seems to have been the result of the work of Apollos in Corinth?

    B. Name and describe the groups of the Corinthian Church:
        1. For what teaching would each group stand?
        2. Which of the groups would be most progressive?
        3. Which would be most conservative?
        4. What would the "party of Christ" represent in the church?

    C. How did Paul show the foolishness of divisions in the church? (Chapter 1:1217)

    D. Why was Paul glad to say he had not personally baptized many of them?

    E. How does Paul reply to the accusation that his gospel is too simple (i.e., not intellectual enough)? (Chapter 2)

    F. Why did Paul choose simple language for them? (Chapter 3)

G. By what two images did Paul show that he and Apollos were not rivals but fellow workers? (Chapter 3)
    1. By what image in the third chapter does he show the relation of a person to God?
    2. Where else in this section does he use the same image?

H. What attitude have the Corinthians apparently taken toward Paul? (Chapter 4)

II.   Immorality in the Church (Chapter 5)

A. What problem should the church be solving rather than quarreling over leaders?

B. What was Paul's command on this and how had it been heeded?

C. Immorality had no more place in the church of Christ than what? (Chapter 5:68)
    1. How effective was this image?

III. Litigation

A. How were the Christians in Corinth settling their disputes?

B. What impressions of the church would this practice give to the gentiles?

C. What should be the spirit and attitude of church members toward each other?

D. If they had quarrels, where and how should they be settled?

Chapter 17
Questions from the Church
Scripture Reference: 1 Corinthians 7

Subject I: Sexual Relations

I.   Sexual Relations (Chapter 7)

   A. Who brought the letter with the questions from the church?
       (1 Corinthians 16–17)

   B. What was the apparent attitude of some in the church
       toward celibacy?

   C. What did Paul recognize as the normal human relationship?

   D. What clue do you find in this chapter concerning Paul's
       own state?

   E. What would be Paul's preference concerning marriage of
       the unmarried and the widows?

       1. Did he make this a command of Christ?

       2. What was his advice to these people?
   F. What was Paul's attitude toward divorce?

       1. Suppose a mixed marriage between a Christian and a
           pagan were happy, what would Paul say about divorce?

       2. If such a marriage were unhappy, what would Paul say?

       3. Who should take steps to do what Paul advised,
           and why?

4. What would Paul probably say about originating a marriage between a Christian and a pagan?

G. Would Paul permit the marriage of women who had taken the vow of virginity?

1. Explain this practice.

2. Do we have anything comparable to this in modern times?

H. What two arguments against marriage did Paul make? (Chapter 7:25–35)

I. How true was his statement that the unmarried person has "more time for the Lord"?

J. What should a man do in regard to his unmarried daughter?

K. In these problems of personal relationships, was Paul giving commands or advice?

L. If the question of chastity were at stake, would Paul command or advise, and what?

Chapter 18
Questions from the Church Continued
Scripture Reference: 1 Corinthians 8–11

Subject II: Meat Offered to Idols

I.   What was done with the surplus meat that had been offered to idols?

     A. How could a gentile get this meat?

     B. If he ate it, what effect would it have on his religious belief?

II.   Where could one obtain the best meat? Why?
     A. Should a Christian buy this meat?

     B. Suppose he realized that there was only one god, and that this meat which had been offered in the temple of a pagan deity was unaffected by the sacrifice, could he eat it?

     C. How about the man who could not get away from the idea that the meat had been offered to idols?

     D. What danger might further eating of such meat bring?

     E. Suppose the eating of this meat by the strong-minded man made a weaker man also eat it, with the result that he was pulled toward idol worship: What is the obligation of the strong?

III.   Did Paul think that eating idol meat was a sin in itself?

IV.   What arguments did Paul give to show that a man had a logical right to do as he pleased?

A. What consideration more important than individual right should govern the Christian?

B. How had Christ reacted toward his individual right?

C. What example did Paul give of subordinating personal rights to a greater purpose in chapter 9:24–27?

V. When the Israelites played with idols in the wilderness, what happened to them?

    A. What advice did Paul give to the strong in this connection?

    B. What danger toward polytheism did Paul see in the eating of idol meat?

VI. Suppose a Christian was invited to a feast, what would he/she do about the meat?
    A. Which would harm his/her religion more—to eat without questioning, or to create a scene by questioning the source of the meat?

    B. Suppose someone told him/her that the meat served at the table had been offered to idols; what should the Christian do?

    C. Should this be made conspicuous?

VII. What general principle did Paul lay down to govern Christian conduct in this chapter?

Subject III: Abuses in the Church's Worship

I. What was Paul's idea of the position of women?

II. What were the women of the Corinthian church doing?

A. What did the unveiled face and the shorn head symbolize in Corinth?

B. What impression would the gentiles in Corinth receive of the Christian church?

III. What right did Paul have to demand that the Christian women veil their faces, and was this a universal command?

IV. How often was the Lord's Supper observed?

A. How as the food provided for this supper?

B. What abuse had risen from this practice?

V. What had the people of Corinth forgotten about the Lord's Supper?

A. How did Paul correct this?

B. Where did Paul receive his knowledge of the Last Supper of Jesus?

VI. How did Paul change the Lord's Supper from a feast to a ceremonial rite?

Chapter 19
Questions from the Church Continued
Scripture Reference: 1 Corinthians 12–14

Subject IV: Spiritual Gifts

I.   What did the Christians mean by "spiritual gifts"?

II.   When did they think these "gifts" were received?

III.   Did becoming a Christian:

    A. —give a person new faculties and powers?

    B. —through consecration of the person to the church, make possible the development of powers which the person already possessed?

IV.   List the "spiritual gifts" mentioned in 12:4–11.

    A. How were the Christians arranging them?

    B. Which did they think were the most important?

    C. Why?

V.   By what image did Paul show that all the gifts were needed in the church?

VI.   What, in Paul's mind, was the "most excellent way" of all?

    A. What was needed with every gift?

    B. Of the spiritual gifts, which did Paul consider most important? (14:1–5)

C. What would be Paul's preference between Prophecy and Tongues? (14:19)

   1. Suppose all spoke in tongues at once—what impression would be made upon strangers?
   2. In giving his decision concerning the gift of tongues (14:27–28), how many would Paul allow to speak in tongues at one meeting?
   3. How many at one time?
   4. What if there was no interpreter present?
   5. In that case, what should the person who wished to speak in tongues do?

VII. What advice did Paul give to the women?

A. Would he give the same advice today?

B. Why?

Chapter 20
Questions from the Church Continued
Scripture Reference: 1 Corinthians 15

Subject V: The Resurrection

I.   What attitude did the Greeks take toward the resurrection? (Acts 17:32)

II.   List the proofs Paul offered for the resurrection of Christ. (15:11)

III.   What is involved in the denial of the resurrection of Christ?

       A. 15:14–15:

       B. 15:18–19:

IV.   Of what is the resurrection of Christ pledge?

V.   What question did Paul raise regarding the relation of his sufferings and resurrection?

VI.   By what three analogies did Paul assume we could reasonably expect God to provide a body for us at the resurrection? (15:35–41)

       A.

       B.

       C.

VII.   Did Paul believe in the resurrection of the body? Give your reasoning.

VIII. What is the connection of 1 Corinthians 15:42–58 with the rest of the chapter?

    A. Outline Paul's argument here.
      1.
      2.
      3.
      4.

    B. Why is this passage so frequently read at Easter and at funerals?

Chapter 21
Second Corinthians Overview
Scripture Reference: 2 Corinthians

I.   Second Corinthians has been called "a full-length portrait" of Paul. Why?

II.   What had the people of Corinth apparently said about Paul's personal appearance? (10:10)—and about his manner? (10:1; 11:7)

III.   What was Paul's reply? (11:14, 30; 12:10)

IV.   What had they said about Paul's speech? (10:10; 11:6)

V.   What was Paul's defense? (11:6)

VI.   How had they taken his statement concerning his apostleship in 1 Corinthians 15:9?

       (See 2 Corinthians 12:11)

VII.   What had they said about his credentials? (3:1)

VIII.   Describe Paul's letters of recommendation.

IX.   What had they said about Paul's teaching? Consider separately:
—2:17

       —4:3, 5

       —11:4

X.   What had they said about Paul's character? Consider separately:
—1:17

—5:13

—8:20, 21

—10:2

—10:10

—10:15

—12:7-11

—12:16

XI.   Where do we find Paul's most extended account of the suffering which he endured in his ministry? And what had he suffered?

XII.   What general rule did Paul propose for the collection of alms? (See 1 Corinthians 16)

XIII. What motives did Paul offer to the Corinthians for receiving the collection in:
       —2 Corinthians 8:1–5?

       —8:7a?

       —8:7b?

       —8:9?

       —9:2-6?

       —9:6-11?

       —9:12-14?

       —9:15

Chapter 22
Paul's Letter to the Romans Introduction
Scripture References: Acts 20:1, 2; Romans

I. Where did Paul go from Ephesus?

II. At what city in Greece did Paul evidently spend three months?

III. Where does Romans stand in order of writing?
—Why do you think it is placed at the beginning of Paul's letters?

IV. By whom was the church at Rome founded?
—What does the Roman Catholic Church say about this?

—Did Paul have a hand in its founding?

—How could it have been formed?

V. List the reasons given by scholars for the writing of the letter to the Romans.

VI. On the occasion for the letter:
A. Was this a compendium of Paul's teaching? If so, how complete was it?

B. Is Romans a polemic against the gentiles?

C. What reason can you find in Romans 15:22–24 for its writing?

D. From the arguments, would you say that Romans was an epistle or a letter? Why?

VII. What is the nature of the following passages?
 —Romans 15:5

 —15:13

 —15:33

 —16:20

 —16:25-27

 A. Where does Paul usually employ this type of verse?

 B. What does this suggest in regard to the integrity of the book?

 C. Some old manuscripts have blank spaces instead of some of these passages. Does that fact affect your decision?

VIII. After studying the names in chapter 16, to what church would you think the chapter was written? Why?

IX. The scribe who wrote the letter for Paul sends his greeting. Who was he? (Chapter 16)

Chapter 23
Romans; Justification by Faith
Scripture Reference: Romans 1–8

I.   What is Paul's estimate of the moral conditions of the gentile world?

II.   Although the gentiles did not know the God of the Jews, in what ways had God been made visible to them? (1:18–23)

III. What is the moral condition of the Jews?

      A. Upon what have they based their hope for salvation?

      B. What advantage did the Jew have over the gentile? (3:2)

IV.   How did Paul rank the Jews and gentiles in condemnation? (3:9, 23)

V.   If people have sunk so low that they cannot help themselves, how can they attain salvation?

      A. What theological phrase expresses this? (3:28)

VI.   Older theological writings have pictured the death of Christ as an attempt on the part of the Son to persuade God, who is angry at sinners, to forgive them.

      A. How many indications can you find which suggest that the work of redemption was begun by God, rather than the Son? (List chapter and verse from Romans 3–8)

      B. In the theological framework above, why was the Law given?

VII. Romans 7 is believed to be an account of Paul's own struggle with the Law. Describe it.

VIII. What other letter have we studied which deals with the same problem as Romans?

Chapter 24
Romans; Rejection of Jesus by the Jews
Scripture Reference: Romans 9–16

I.   Find definitions for the following terms used by Paul:

   salvation

   justification by faith

   adoption

   reconciliation

   atonement

   propitiation

   sanctification

   redemption

   ransom

   regeneration

II.   What was Paul's concern for the Jews?

III.   In what instances did Paul show that God selects people to suit particular purposes? (Chapter 9)

IV.   By what figure does Paul show God's absolute power over people?

V. When considering salvation, what distinction did Paul think God would make between the Jew and the gentile?

—What verse shows this?

VI. Regarding Jesus as Messiah, who had done the rejecting: God or the Jews?

—Why did this happen? (11:11–12)

VII. By what illustration did Paul attempt to show God's relationship to people? (11:17–24)

—Who were represented by the olive branches broken off?

—Who were meant by the olive branches grafted in?

—Suppose the wild olive branches became boastful, what would happen?

—Suppose the original olive branches should become fruitful in belief, what would happen?

—Does the illustration suggest Paul was a man of the country or the city?

—Why or why not?

VIII. By what figure did Paul make a plea for a personal relationship with God? (Chapter 12)

IX. What practical demands for Christian living did Paul make?

Chapter 25
Journey to Jerusalem and Arrest
Scripture Reference: Acts 20:3–22:30

I.   What change did Paul make in his plans for leaving Greece?

        —Why?

II.   What seven men were to accompany him to Jerusalem?

        —What required such a large committee?

        —Where did these men plan to meet Paul?

        —Why did they not go with him by land?

III.   Who joined Paul's company at Philippi?

        —How do you know?

IV.   Tell the story of the meeting at Troas.

        —What near tragedy happened there?

V.   Why did Paul stop at Miletus instead of Ephesus?

        —For what purpose did he stop there?

        —How final was his farewell to the elders?

        —Did Paul anticipate trouble ahead?

        —How do you know?

VI.   What plea did Paul's friends in Tyre make to him?

VII.   What was the exhortation of Philip's daughters?

VIII. How did Agabus show Paul that it was not safe for him to go to Jerusalem?

IX.   How did Paul reply to these pleadings?

      —Was he right in going to Jerusalem under the circumstances?

      —Why do you think this?

X.   Trace the Third Missionary Journey on an outline map.

XI.   What was the feeling of the Jews and Jewish Christians at Jerusalem toward Paul?

      —How did the leaders of the church suggest that Paul might appeal to the Jews?

      —How long did the purification ceremony last?

XII.   Who stirred up the people against Paul?

      —What accusation did they make against him? Was it true?

      —What did they plan to do with Paul?

      —How did Paul escape?

XIII. Who did the Roman centurion think Paul was?

      —What was the centurion's name? (23:26)

XIV. What request did Paul make of the captain?

    —In what language did Paul speak to the captain?

    —In what language did he speak to the Jews?

XV. What was in the speech of Paul which angered the Jews?

XVI. Tell the story of how Paul's Roman citizenship helped him in the castle.

XVII. Which of the men had the most prized citizenship? Why?

Chapter 26
The Trial of Paul at Jerusalem and Caesarea
Scripture Reference: Acts 23:1–26:32

I.   Before what body was Paul tried in Jerusalem?

     A. Who composed this body?

     B. What religion did this body represent?

     C. What religion did Paul represent?

II.   How did Paul protest the fact that he was brought for trial before this body?

     A. What did the authorities demand be done to Paul?

     B. Why did Paul not know that it was a person in authority who made the demand?

III.   What did the makeup of the body have to do with Paul' statement about resurrection?

     A. How did the statement affect the body?

     B. How did the trial end?

IV.   What vow did certain Jews make concerning Paul?

     A. How was the vow frustrated?

V.   Who was governor of Caesarea when Paul was brought for trial?

     A. What kind of man was he?

VI. Who came from Jerusalem to accuse Paul?

    A. What four accusations did he bring against Paul? [24:5, 6]

    B. How did Paul answer these accusations? [24:11–21]

VII. What verdict did the Governor pronounce?

VIII. Why was Paul kept in prison and for how long?

IX. What did the Governor do with Paul when he returned to Rome? Why?

X. Who was the succeeding Governor?

    A. What request did the leaders at Jerusalem make of him?

    B. What did they plan to do?

XI. How did Paul escape being sent to Jerusalem for trial?

    A. What was the meaning of his act?

XII. To whom did Festus present Paul for trial?

    A. What predicament was Festus in? (25:26)

XIII. What impression did Paul's speech make upon Agrippa?

    A. Do you think Agrippa was being sarcastic, or was he sincere?

XIV. What was Agrippa's verdict?

Chapter 27
The Trip to Rome
Scripture Reference: Acts 27, 28

I.   Who was Paul's guard for this transport of prisoners and what friends accompanied him?

II.   Where did the ship embark for Rome?

    A. What was the intended route?

    B. What route did they actually take?

    C. Why?

III.   Where did Paul advise the ship owner to spend the winter?

    A. Where did the owner want to winter over?

    B. What was the outcome?

    C. What emergency measures were taken? (27:16–19)

    D. Describe Paul's part in the experiences of the next two weeks.

IV.   How did the crew and passengers discover that they were nearing the shore?

    A. How did they prevent the ship from being driven upon the rocks?

    B. What did the sailors plan to do?

    C. What did Paul advise?

    D. How many people were on the ship?

    E. Why was Paul certain they would be saved?

V.   Why did the soldiers plan to kill the prisoners?

VI.   Why did the Centurion refuse?

VII. On what island was the boat shipwrecked?

    A. What is the modern name for this island?

    B. What was the attitude of the inhabitants toward the shipwrecked men?

VIII. Tell the story of Paul's experience on the shore.

    A. What did the people think of him as a result?

    B. What service did Paul render to the people of the island?

    C. Did he have anyone to help him?

IX.   How did Paul get on to Rome?

X.   Why did Paul call the Jews to him when he reached Rome?

    A. What was the result of the interview?

    B. Where did Paul stay while in Rome?

    C. For how long?

XI.   Who was the Roman Emperor at this time?

      A. What was he like?

      B. What was his attitude toward Christians?

      C. What important Christian practice developed rapidly in Rome under Nero?

XII.   Trace the route of this trip on a map.

Chapter 28
The Letter to Philemon
Scripture Reference: Philemon

I.   Where was Paul when he wrote this letter?

II.   What references show where he was?

III.   Who was Philemon? (Philemon 1, 2; Colossians 4:17)

IV.   Who were Apphia and Archippus, and where did they live?

V.   Who was Onesimus?

     A. What had he done?

     B. Where had Paul found him?

     C. What had he done for Paul?

     D. What had Paul done for him?

     E. What did Paul persuade Onesimus to do after his conversion?

     F. What pun did Paul make on the name of Onesimus? (v. 11)

VI.   Describe the condition and treatment of slaves in the Mediterranean world at this time.

VII.   What treatment could the slave in this letter expect?

VIII. Why did Paul write to Philemon?

     A. What previous acquaintance had Paul had with Philemon? (v. 19)

B. What special consideration did Paul request?

C. What did Paul promise?

D. What debt does Paul imply that Philemon owes him?

IX. What suggestion is there in this letter that Paul expects to be set free and return East?

X. Did Paul attack the institution of slavery in this letter?

XI. Did Paul ask that the slave be set free?

XII. What kind of slavery did Paul preach against?

XIII. If all Christians treated their slaves as Paul suggested, what would be the end result?

Chapter 29
The Letter to the Phlippians
Scripture reference: Philippians

I.   Where was Paul when he wrote this letter?

    A. What indication do we have that he was in prison?

    B. 1:12–18 indicates that something has happened to Paul—
        1.   What is it?
        2.   What is Paul's status now?
        3.   What effect has this had on preaching the gospel?
        4.   What fate would Paul choose for himself if he could?

II.   What had the people of Philippi done for Paul? (4:15–18)

    A. Who was the messenger?

    B. What happened to the messenger? (2:25–30)

    C. What had the church at Philippi evidently done? (2:26)

    D. What had Paul evidently neglected that he was correcting by writing this letter?

III.   What indication is there in 2:19ff that Paul expects a new trial?

    A. How does he expect it to end?

    B. Who will be sent as soon as Paul knows the decision?

    C. What is his own hope?

IV.   Why is Paul's letter to the Philippians:

    A. called his "love letter"?

B. called his "joy letter"?

C. Find one minor criticism Paul makes of the Philippian Church.

V. Find the most-often-quoted verse of Philippians.

VI. What does Paul mean, "Have this mind in you, which was in Christ Jesus?" (2:5)

A. What did Paul say Jesus had the right to claim? (2:6)

B. What did Jesus do instead?

C. What was God's response to his act? (2:9–11)

D. What does this passage imply about the pre-existence of Christ?

Chapter 30
The Letter to the Colossians
Scripture Reference: Colossians

I.   Where was Colossae?

    A. What other two cities were nearby?

    B. Describe the area where they are located.

    C. For what were these three cities noted? (Revelation 3:14–22)

II.   Who probably founded the church at Colossae? (1:7)

    A. Had Paul been there? (2:1)

    B. What was the occasion for this letter?

    C. How was the need communicated to Paul?

    D. How was the letter sent back? (4:7ff)

III. Who were the Jewish Essenes?

    A. What were their beliefs and practices?

    B. Is there any indication that they might have caused trouble in Colossae?

IV.   What is Gnosticism?

    A. What ideas of creation and mediation did the Gnostics hold?

    B. Do you find any indications that the Gnostic problem was speculative?

C. According to the Gnostics, what was the only way a person could be saved?

D. What did the false teachers say about Christ as a mediator?

E. How did they rank Christianity with their own religion?

V. Did Paul acknowledge Christ as incomplete either in position or in function?

   A. Did he consider Christ merely as an intermediary being? (1:15–2:9)

   B. What does he say about Christ as mediator?

   C. What relation does Christ hold to creation? (1:16; 2:10)

   D. By what name does Paul speak of angels?

VI. By his claim on behalf of Christ, what did Paul leave for the Gnostics?

VII. What would be the impact of this letter on believers in Colossae?

VIII. What would be the impact on the heresies?

IX. How does Paul condemn the Gnostic teachings? (2:8, 18)

X. What image does Paul use to show the relation of Christ to His Church?

XI. What type of moral living did Gnostic teaching produce?

XII. By comparison, what did Paul demand of Christians?

XIII. What do we mean by the "Colossae Code?" (3:18–4:1)

XIV. Colossians is called the "ALL" letter.

A. Why?

B. List references from chapters 1–3 to justify this name.

Chapter 31
Paul's Letter to the Ephesians
Scripture Reference: Ephesians

I.   Remembering Paul's three years spent in Ephesus, what do the following passages suggest about whether this letter was intended for the Ephesian Church?

    A. 1:15

    B. 3:2–5

    C. 4:21

II.   How might the letter have become known as the letter to the Ephesians?

III.   Discuss the similarity between Ephesians and Colossians.

IV.   What image for the relations of Christ to the Church is found in Colossians and expounded at length in Ephesians?

V.   In Ephesians, what has been done with the "Household Code" of Colossians?

VI.   The keynote of Ephesians is found in 4:1–7. What is it?

VII.   What outstanding series of images did Paul use in the last chapter?

VIII. What was he trying to say with the use of those images?

IX.   Who carried this letter to its destination?

X.   X What connection did the bearer have with the letter to the Colossians?

Chapter 32
Paul's Pastoral Letters
Scripture References (read in this order):
1 Timothy, Titus, 2 Timothy

I.   Why are these called Pastoral Letters?

II. Where in the book of Acts can you find the historical references listed below?

   A. 1 Timothy 1:3—When was this?

   B. 2 Timothy 4:13—If Paul left them on his way to Jerusalem, wouldn't he have needed them before four years of imprisonment?

   C. 2 Timothy 4:20a—When was this?

   D. 2 Timothy 4:20b—Did Paul leave Trophimus ill at Miletus, on his way to Jerusalem? (See Acts 21:29)

   E. Titus 1:5—When did Paul found the church at Crete?

   F. Titus 3:12—When was this plan made?

III. If Paul wrote these letters, did he write them before or after the close of Acts?

IV. If we accept the Pastorals as Paul's, what must we think about a second imprisonment?

V.   What possibility is there that Paul was freed at Rome?

   A. What negative argument is present in the ending of Acts?

B. Was the charge in Philippians 1:12ff sufficient for the death penalty?

C. What did Paul expect in the prison letters? [Philemon 22; Philippians 2:24]

D. What is the tradition about Paul's journey to Spain and his death in Rome?

E. What do the references in question II suggest?

VI.   The authenticity of the Pastorals is bound up in what fact?

VII. What argument for date is made in regard to church organization?

VIII. What argument is made in regard to style and vocabulary?

IX.   What argument is made in regard to Paul's attitude toward Timothy?

X.   Some suggest that Paul was planning to leave the east forever and that he was giving his authority over to Timothy and Titus. Would that be a satisfactory explanation of the details?

XI.   What kind of man would you suppose Timothy to be from 1 Timothy? (Recall that he had carried a letter to the Corinthians and that Paul had had to send a bitter letter before the situation was healed.) (1 Corinthians 1:10, 11; 2 Corinthians 7:5–9)

XII. What would you suggest as the keynote of 2 Timothy?

A. What is Paul's personal condition? What has happened to him?

B. What does he expect will happen?

C. What has happened to the friends and followers of Paul?

D. What is Paul's last request of Timothy?

XIII. How does Titus compare with Timothy in strength of character? (Judge from the letter to Titus and 2 Corinthians 8:16–24.)

XIV. What is Paul's "Swan Song?"

XV. What was the fate of Paul according to the Church Fathers?

DATES

YEAR	EGYPT	GREECE	PALESTINE	ITALY–PERSIA
3400 BC		Age of Cretans til 1400 BC		
3000 BC	Upper and Lower Egypt united			
2776 BC	Egyptian calendar invented			
1750 BC	Hyksons Conquer Egypt			
1600 BC	The Empire til 1200 BC			
1500 BC		Mycenaean Age til 1200 BC		
1020 BC			Israel united as a nation under Saul	
1025 BC			David becomes King	
940 BC			Hebrew Kingdom divided	Assyria begins to expand
900 BC		Age of Homer		
842 BC			Assyria controls Israel	
800 BC		Greek kingdoms overthrown		
722 BC			Fall of Northern Kingdom to Assyria	
672 BC		Assyrians conquer Egypt		
650 BC				Etruscans in Italy til 509 BC

YEAR	EGYPT	GREECE	PALESTINE	ITALY–PERSIA
621 BC		Rise of Greek city states		
		(Draco's Code)		
606 BC			Assyria falls to Babylon	
586 BC			Fall of Southern Kingdom to Babylon (Exile)	

YEAR	EGYPT	GREECE	PALESTINE	ITALY-PERSIA
525 BC	Egypt's power ends		Persians take Egypt	
509 BC	Founding of Roman Republic			
461 BC	Athenian Empire til 404 BC			
404 BC	Spartan Empire til 371 BC			
338 BC	Philip II conquers Greece			
336 BC	Alexander the Great til 323 BC			
325 BC				Italy conquered by 265 BC
323 BC	Greeks rule Palestine til 63 BC			
196 BC		Fall of Seleucid Greek Empire		
167 BC			Great Persecution of Jews til 164 BC	
166 BC			Maccabean Revolt, Jewish independence til 63 BC	
163 BC			Essene Community formed at Qumran	
146 BC		Rome takes Greece		
63 BC			Romans take Palestine	
44 BC		Death of Julius Caesar		
31 BC		Rome takes Egypt		
27 BC		Octavian establishes Roman Empire—reigns as Augustus til AD 14		

til AD 37

YEAR	EGYPT	GREECE	PALESTINE	ITALY	PERSIA
4(6?) BC			Birth of Jesus		
AD 14		Tiberius reigns			
AD 31			Crucifixion of Jesus		
AD 54			Nero reigns til AD 68		
AD 70			Destruction of Jerusalem by Rome		
AD 98		Trajan reigns til AD 117			
AD 117				Hadrian reigns til AD 138	
AD 161		Marcus Aurelius reigns til AD 180			
AD 235		Roman Empire Falters til AD 284			
AD 284		Diocletian reigns til AD 305			
AD 303		Last Christian persecutions til AD 311			
AD 325				Council of Nicaea	
AD 323		Constantine reigns til AD 337, moves to Constantinople and recognizes Christianity			
AD 410			Sack of Rome by the Goths		
AD 440			Pope Leo the Great til AD 461		

YEAR	EGYPT	GREECE	PALESTINE	ITALY	PERSIA
AD 476		End of Roman Empire in the West			
AD 527			Justinian reigns in the East til AD 565		

[compiled by Rodney Peters]

Appendix

A Chronology of Paul's Life and Work

Nearly all dates given here are called into question by someone. This chronology is not offered as a definitive statement about the exact sequence or times of events in Paul's life and work. Rather, it is intended to provide a general framework within which a close reading of the materials can be pursued. In the midst of study, discussion, and debate, the precise truth of events may never be found—but the power of the Holy Spirit will be experienced.

Anno Domini 10

> Born Saul at Tarsus in Cilicia of a Jewish family of the tribe of Benjamin
> Roman citizen, raised in a predominately Greek culture
> Educated with a Pharisaic view of scripture and religion, under Gamaliel in Jerusalem

AD 34

> Struck temporarily blind by a vision of Christ on the road from Jerusalem to Damascus
> Responding to the call of Christ, went to Arabia for a time, then back to Jerusalem

AD 39

> Having returned to Tarsus and the region of Syria and Cilicia, called by the Christians in Antioch of Syria (through Barnabas) to serve them

AD 45

> Commissioned (with Barnabas) as a missionary by the Christian Church of Antioch

AD 45–49
> The First Missionary Campaign

AD 49
> The Council of Jerusalem

AD 50–51
> Wrote to the Thessalonians

AD 50–52
> The Second Missionary Campaign

AD 53–58
> The Third Missionary Campaign

AD 56–57
> Wrote to the Philippians

AD 57
> Wrote to the Corinthians

AD 57–58
> Wrote to the Romans and Galatians

AD 58
> Arrested in Jerusalem

AD 58–60
> Imprisoned at Caesarea in Palestine

AD 60
> Sent to Rome under guard at the order of Festus

AD 61–63

 Lived in Rome, in prison or under house arrest all the time
 Wrote to the Ephesians and Colossians
 Wrote to Philemon

(From AD 63 on, the chronology of Paul's life is largely speculative.)

AD 63

 Perhaps released from prison for lack of evidence, possibly traveling east to Spain

AD 65

 Traditional date for writing 1 Timothy and Titus (for those who consider them Pauline)

AD 66–67

 Traditional date for writing 2 Timothy, during a new imprisonment

AD 67

 Traditional date for Paul's martyrdom in Rome

Bibliography

Bailey, Kenneth E. *Paul Through Mediterranean Eyes: Cultural Studies in 1 Corinthians*. Downers Grove, IL: InterVarsity Press, 2011.

Barclay, William. *The Letters to the Philippians, Colossians, and Thessalonians*. Westminster: John Knox Press, 1959.

Crossan, John Dominic and Jonathan L. *Reed. In Search of Paul*. New York, NY: Harper Collins, 2005.

Davies, W.D. *Paul and Rabbinic Judaism*. London: SCM Press, 1948.

Deissmann, Adolf. *St. Paul: A Study in Social and Religious History*. London: Hodder and Stoughton, 1912.

Goodspeed, Edgar J. *Paul*. Philadelphia and Toronto: The John C. Winston Company, 1947.

Holman Bible Publisher, *Holman Book of Biblical Charts, Maps, and Reconstructions*, 1993.

Hunter, A.M. *The Gospel According to St. Paul*. Guildford and London: Billing and Sons, LTD, 1966.

Tabor, James D. *Paul and Jesus*. New York, NY: Simon & Schuster, 2012.

The New Jerusalem Bible, published and copyright by Darton, Longman and Todd, Ltd, London: 1985.

An overview of the life of Rodney G. Peters

Degrees and Certificates:

2007	Family Mediation Certificate – Missouri State University – Springfield, MO
1990	Stephen Ministry Leadership Certificate – St. Louis. MO
1985-1986	Clinical Pastoral Education Certificate – Wesley Medical Center – Wichita, KS
1982	Graduate Hours in Preaching – Earlham School of Religion – Richmond, IN
1980	Graduate Hours in Sociology – Wichita State University – Wichita, KS
1961-1965	M. Div. /Extra Hours in Christian Education – McCormick Seminary – Chicago, IL
1957-1961	B. A. in Sociology *Summa Cum Laude* – Parsons College – Fairfield, IA

Continuing Education:

2012	Leadership for Change Conference – Earlham School of Religion – Richmond, IN
2011	Presbyterian USA Big Tent Event – Indianapolis. IN
2007	Mediation Training – Missouri State University – Springfield. MO
2005	National Presbyterian Peacemaking Conference – Ghost Ranch – Abiquiu, NM
1997	David Ray Small Church Pastorate Seminar – John Calvin Presbytery – Carthage, MO
1996	Simple Living Seminar – Little Portion Monastery – Eureka Springs, AR
1995	Church History Independent Study – England and Northern Ireland

1993	National Presbyterian Peacemaking Conference – Estes Park, CO
1992	Synod School of Mid-America – Central Missouri State University – Warrensburg, MO
1991	School for Pastors – University of Dubuque/Hastings College – Hastings, NE
1991	Synod School of Mid-America – Central Missouri State University – Warrensburg, MO
1991	Antagonistic People in the Church Workshop – Spiritual Life Center – Wichita, KS
1991	Church Planning for Families Workshop/Dr. Cynthia Pellet – Wichita, KS
1991	P. R. for Non-profit Organizations– Public Relations Society of America – Wichita, KS
1990	Peacemaking 2000 Conference – American University – Washington, DC
1984-1989	112 Approved Contact Training Hours – KS Dept. of Adult and Child Care Facilities
1984	Writers' Workshop/Roland Tapp – Montreat Conference Center – Montreat, NC
1983	Pastors' School – Omaha Seminary Foundation/ Hastings College – Hastings, NE
1977	Graduate Conference on Current Economics – Iowa Council on Economic Education/University of Iowa – Iowa City, IA
1976	Small Church Workshop/Dr. Robert Worley, Dr. Carl Dudley – McCormick Theological Seminary – Chicago, IL
1976	Omaha School for Pastors – Omaha Seminary Foundation/University of Nebraska at Omaha – Omaha, NE
1976	Congregational Planning Training Event/Dr. Richard Miller –

	Presbyteries of North Central and Northwest IA – Mason City, IA
1975	Death and the Dying Patient Conference/Dr. Elizabeth Kubler-Ross –
	Wartburg College – Waverly, IA
1973	Piaget and Open Education Conference/Dr. David Elkind –
	Chicago Association for the Education of Young Children – Chicago, IL

Teaching History:

2011	Workshop Leader, Heartland Presbytery A.P.C.E. Event, "Sunday School On Call"
	(Multiple Years) Planning Team of the Middle America
	(Multiple Years) Instructor, Wee Kirk Conference held in Wagoner, OK

1986–Forward, Frequent seminar leader, lecturer, and teacher in churches, for religious organizations, and for the Presbyterian denomination

1986	Workshop Leader, Synod of Mid-America, "Focus: Ministry and Aging – Spirituality"
1984	Workshop Leader, Kansas Association of Chaplains, "Retiring Whole and Well"
1976–1980	Workshop Leader, North Central Iowa Presbytery
	"Facilitating Congregational Self-Assessment"
	"Toward Improving Ministry"
1965–1973	Administrator and Consultant/Early Childhood Education in the Church
	First Presbyterian Church Nursery School, Jackson, MI
	First Presbyterian Church Nursery School, Oak Park, IL
	Oak Park Free School (Elementary), Oak Park, IL
	Village Day Care Center, Oak Park, IL

1970	Workshop Leader, National College of Education, Evanston, IL
	"Youth Crisis Intervention"
1969–1970	Honors Program Instructor, "Medical Ethics"
	Northwestern University Medical School/Chicago Campus, Chicago, IL

Employment History:

2015–2018	Pastor, First Presbyterian Church, Scammon, KS (Supply)
2004–2015	Pastor, Bethany Presbyterian Church, Joplin MO (half-time, Stated Supply)
1992–2004	Pastor, Crane Presbyterian Church, Crane, MO
1989–1992	Associate Pastor for Congregational Life and Evangelism
	Grace Presbyterian Church, Wichita, KS
1988–1989	Interim Pastor, West Side Presbyterian Church, Wichita, KS
1983–1988	Chaplain, Wichita Presbyterian Manor, Wichita, KS
1980–1985	Pastor, First Presbyterian Church, Conway Spring, KS (half-time)
	Home Improvements Business Owner, Conway Springs, KS (half-time)
1973–1980	Pastor, Unity and Community Parish, Clarksville, IA
1967–1973	Associate Pastor for Christian Education
	First Presbyterian Church, Oak Park, IL
1965–1967	Assistant Pastor for Christian Education
	First Presbyterian Church, Jackson, MI

Printed in the United States
by Baker & Taylor Publisher Services